How to Advance in the Kingdom of Heaven –

While battling with the sin nature

Kingdom Publishers

How to Advance in the Kingdom of Heaven
Copyright© Colin Elliott

ISBN: 978-1-913247-76-8

1st Edition by Kingdom Publishers
Kingdom Publishers
London, UK.

You can purchase copies of this book from any leading bookstore or
email **contact@kingdompublishers.co.uk**

Dedication

To my wife for her support, insightful comments and patience
while editing this book and to my daughters who were
a source of inspiration and encouragement.
Thank you Tanya, a sister in Christ who encouraged me
to write this book.

Contents

*Hope is at hand for you to enjoy your life right now,
in the midst of life's storms.*

The Author

COLIN ELLIOTT is a trained and experienced volunteer Christian counsellor, who has been providing emotional and spiritual support to brothers and sisters in Christ, as well as those seeking to learn more about Christianity, for over twenty years.

"Your life can experience such freedom and liberty based on God's word as found in the scriptures which will help you grow in confidence in your walk, indeed your fellowship with Christ.

It is my sincere hope that within these pages a comfort in God's love will be found. For all who desire to experience this comfort as part of their life today, and should this be you dear reader,– read on!"

Colin Elliott

'From the time John the Baptist began preaching until now, the kingdom of heaven has been forcefully advancing...'

(Matthew 11:12 NLT)

Introduction

Many good, well intentioned Christians are physically and mentally exhausted due to not knowing how to function on a daily basis in a way that is pleasing to God, while battling sin. The effects of sin are all around us and within us; and a lack or misunderstanding of the scriptures can leave us vulnerable to a false perception of the faith, leaving us feeling guilty and frustrated as we try to resolve the same problems over and over again, without realising that a way out has already been made for us, through Christ Jesus.

Whether you are someone who has started the journey, but constantly find yourself stumbling, or a mature Christian who feels like giving up, this book will help you to identify futile habits and ways of thinking which can frustrate your Christian walk and growth; as you battle daily against the person you were, while walking toward who you are becoming in Christ.

This book will also encourage you to enjoy the journey of faith by highlighting common pitfalls that can frustrate your spiritual growth, while encouraging you to run the course set out for you, secure in the knowledge that '...there is now no condemnation for those who are in Christ Jesus...' (Romans 8:1 NIV) and, in spite of your weaknesses, you are loved with a bond that can never be broken.

Chapter 1

Two reputations – One in heaven

What God has called you to do, that good work, must be a priority in your life. When Nehemiah faced opposition to the rebuilding of the walls of Jerusalem, he maintained his focus on God's priority and sent a beautifully worded reply to those deliberately scheming to harm him and frustrate the rebuilding process, *'I am carrying on a great project and cannot go down. Why should the work stop while I leave it and go down to you?'* (Nehemiah 6:3 NIV).

As Christians we are conscious of a new life and seek to honour the Lord in what we do, and refusing others can be difficult. However, sometimes 'NO', is a valid answer. We should not be frightened to tell others, particularly those who previously despised our following the Lord, No! They see now that your way is peaceful and yielding fruit in accord with scriptural promises and that you are a more responsible person. Moreover, in many cases their request can be based on a selfish motive, for their own benefit, regardless of the cost or outcome to you. Of course we don't have to be rude, that is not who we are, but we can be firm.

Such dedication immediately makes us fall out of favour with worldly views and priorities. This applies in nearly every aspect of our daily lives, from the home to the workplace. We are '*in*' the world, but not '*of*' it, and when we choose the kingdom's value system, we automatically challenge this world's value system. The consequence of our obedience to God therefore, leaves us with two reputations based on our actions, one in heaven known to God and one here on earth seen and commented on by the world.

As much as we are told to seek peace, this can be very often illusive, especially when challenging widely accepted views and practices. The temptation is to compromise a little or even quit, so as to be accepted. This is not to say that there are no grey areas in life that can't be discussed, debated and are needful of prayer. In these situations God's grace is sufficient to cover us, even when we make a mistake. He will guide us and help us to use our liberty in prosperous ways.

We must always keep in mind that God's ways are leading us into freedom and purpose, as opposed to bondage and futility. This means that you may well be viewed by many, including some in the church, as wrong. To stand for truth is costly and your earthly reputation may well be tarnished. This is painful; I don't believe that anybody really enjoys being disliked, but being disliked or even hated may well be the price we pay sometimes for just standing firm in what we believe.

Jesus knows exactly what we are experiencing, because he himself took the full weight of rejection and sin for our sake, so that we would '*...not grow weary and lose heart.*' (Hebrews 12:3 NIV). It is to our glory and joy that we are '*...sharing in his sufferings...*' (Philippians 3:10 NIV) in the heavenly realm, our reputation is glorious. We are counted worthy and known by God as those precious to him. We are told in Philippians that Jesus '...*made himself of no reputation...*' (Philippians 2:7 KJV) and how God exalted him because of his obedience and humility. He will do the same for us.

In the life of Jesus, we can see the effects of following God in total obedience. The attacks against him were relentless. His character was called into question by the religious leaders and Pharisees, who were not beyond insulting him. They would also seek to undermine him in public and attack his reputation, as when they brought to him the woman caught in the act of adultery.

On another occasion while visiting the house of a Pharisee, Jesus was not even afforded the common courtesy of being offered water to wash his feet. This honour was left to a woman despised by the religious as being a sinner, but loved by God. Moreover, in her act of wetting the feet of Christ with her tears and drying them with her hair, she was indeed blessed.

To function in the presence of such hostility, Jesus demonstrated the power of a close one-to-one relationship with the Father. In spite of all that man could do against him, he was secure in the Father's love, to the point that when many of his followers, troubled with his teachings began to desert him, he asked the twelve disciples if they wanted to go also, to which Peter replied '*Lord, to whom shall we go? You have the words of eternal life.*' (John 6:68 NIV).

Our personal time in communion with our heavenly Father is crucial if we are to successfully benefit from our heavenly reputation, and walk confidently in it. During these times God will guide you and also let you know how much he loves you. If you are living for the Lord and seeking to glorify him in your life, I can guarantee you that the world won't love you. In fact, I would go as far to say that if you are very popular and well loved by the world, it may well be worth checking your 'kingdom credentials', to see if you are following heaven's blue-print for your life.

Jesus quite clearly lets us know the outcome of our obedience that *'"In this world you will have trouble. But take heart! I have overcome the world."'* (John 16:33 NIV). Now, we don't go looking for trouble, on the contrary we are told to seek peace, but being obedient to the truth revealed in scripture and through the Holy Spirit, is in many ways a declaration of war to much of what the world values and holds dear. If they hated Jesus, and they did, (read John 15:18-25), they will inevitably hate you.

Jeanne Guyon, in her book Song of Songs describes the consequences of our devotion to God this way:

'Those who are beginning to serve God are commonly persecuted by the unregenerate because their withdrawal is a public condemnation of the disorders which reign in the world.'

Justifications, by Jeanne Guyon, p37

Thankfully, this is not the end of the story as Jesus reminds us to take heart in all of life's challenges, for he has overcome the world.

The encouragement and strength Jesus received to fulfil his mission, as a result of his obedience and close communion with the Father, is revealed to us many times in scripture. The testing in the wilderness for forty days and nights, when after the trial the angels came and tended him (Matthew 4:11) or when he spoke to the disciples of having *'...food to eat that you know nothing about.'* (John 4:32 NIV) at Jacob's Well.

There were also many confirmations from the Father and others such as Peter's confession that Jesus is *'...the Christ, the Son of the living God.'* (Matthew 16:16 NKJV), the revelation of which Jesus pointed out came from the Father. Also, coming to the end of his earthly ministry, Jesus was asked by the thief on the cross to *'...remember me when you come into your kingdom.'* (Luke 23:42 NIV). The Son of God was encouraged at key moments in his walk upon the earth, and this is something we all need and will receive, to help us progress in the good works God has prepared in advance for us to do.

Your heavenly Father will supply all your needs for your present and future battles, as well as providing you with scheduled moments of rest, affirmation and encouragement. No matter which earthly foes are against you, whether it be family members, friends or work colleagues, enjoy your life based on what God says about you and not man. The Bible tells us that *'...He who is in you is greater than he who is in the world...'* (1 John 4:4 NKJV).

The apostle Paul in his letter to the Corinthian Church, told them to *'...be ye separate.'* (2 Corinthians 6:17 KJV) In his daily devotional, Morning and Evening, Charles Spurgeon, commenting on this verse reminds us that:

> 'If a thing be right, though you lose by it, it must be done; if it be wrong, though you would gain by it, you must scorn the sin for your Master's sake.'

> (September 11, morning reading)

Given the fact that the brief span of our lives in this world, according to James, is just a 'vapour', we should always keep an eye on eternity. The *'Well done, my good servant!'* (Luke 19:17 NIV) are words of comfort and encouragement we can all receive now, based on our heavenly reputation: *'Blessed are you when people insult you, persecute you and falsely say all kinds of evil against you because of me. Rejoice and be glad, because great is your reward in heaven...'* (Matthew 5:11-12 NIV).

Chapter 2

Trusting God for your future prosperity

During the very intense times of our battle to walk obediently with God, we become very aware of our own weaknesses and the need for God's strength. As I was writing this passage I was in physical pain. Many questions were bouncing around in my head as to why I have to suffer in this way. How can I do anyone any good like this? Moreover, my many previous ailments only seemed to reinforce my weaknesses, not my faith. All my thoughts were on relief and the lack of God's help. I know he can heal, so why am I going through this? All my previous attempts to grow in faith seem to lead me from one trial to the next.

During this time 'hope' was just a four letter word with very little meaning in my life, to the point where I would say to myself 'I want out', or 'I've had enough!' If I were to tell you that I felt any other way, I would be lying to you. My mind was not short of suggestions either, as to how I could temporarily escape from my condition, many of them worldly. Standing back and looking at such situations from a position of faith, I found extremely difficult. I also knew that this is exactly what I had to do.

This is the battle ground of faith for the believer where the *'...weapons of our warfare are not carnal but mighty in God for pulling down strongholds...'* (2 Corinthians 10:4 NKJV). During such times let your hurt be known and continue to seek God. Your honesty in prayer during these times will not alienate you from his presence; we all struggle with difficulties that challenge our faith at times. However, we must strive to ensure that the difficulty does not have the final word on any present circumstance, which is contrary to what God has promised us personally, or through his word.

During such times of being open and honest, I personally believe that we have more chance of throwing a tennis ball to Mars from Earth, than we do of offending the one who loves us more than we love ourselves. The love God has for us is constantly seeking to draw us closer to him in a way that no one else can, *'How priceless is your unfailing love...'* (Psalm 36:7 NIV).

We know that the battle is the Lord's, but the heat of battle is definitely felt by us. The Lord feels it too. It is during these times that we need to press on the hardest, knowing that our righteousness is our breastplate. Ephesians 6 tells us to put on the breastplate of righteousness. The world may not necessarily view us as righteous, but God declares us righteous, based on our saviour's glorious life, death and resurrection. We have already been mightily blessed by the Lord and Luke 12:48 tells us *'...from everyone who has been given much, much will be demanded...'*

The battle always reveals two things, first, God's love and grace towards us during these times; and secondly, our weaknesses. These are purging moments for us that will produce fruits of faith that will encourage us in the future, as well as others who can learn from our experiences.

Moreover, do not be surprised if your enemy seems to be doing well and unhindered, while you, who are fighting for the faith are going through so much hardship, disappointments and maybe even ill health. As difficult as things are, try not to lose focus, keep your eyes on Jesus, the author and perfecter of our faith. Even when things become really challenging, stand firm. This will help us to develop eyes of faith that will enable us to discern the truth behind any future trials God uses to build our character, faith, as well as developing in us a greater dependency on him.

The enemy wants us to focus on him and his lies, and the more you do this, the harder it will become for you to believe anything other than your losing. David, before he became King of Israel felt this way after there were continuous attempts by King Saul to take his life. The Bible records for us David's thoughts during this very difficult time *'One of these days I will be destroyed by the hand of Saul.'* (1 Samuel 27:1 NIV) Do not underestimate the relentless energy of those who are opposed to you and the will of God. At such times those against us almost seem invincible.

This is what caused Elijah to flee from Jezebel. After everything Elijah had done to demonstrate how great God was at Mount Carmel, with the people witnessing the power of God in consuming the sacrifice and the fate of the prophets of Baal, yet still many hearts remained hardened, with Jezebel threatening to take Elijah's life. With opponents so hateful and fired up it is hard to believe that you can win, or that God will be able to deliver you.

This is an illusion put forward by the enemy in such a convincing way, as to undermine your faith and trust in God. What they have done by their actions and words is to get you to focus on their 'power' and in doing so they have robbed you of the joy of all that God has brought you through in the past, in an attempt to cancel your faith in the promises of God regarding your future. This is not the time to retreat, on the contrary, trust firmly by faith that the same God who has delivered you in the past, will continue to give you the victory.

After one of the Union's most discouraging defeats of the American Civil War, Abraham Lincoln wrote in a private reflection on the matter entitled A Meditation on the Divine Will:

'The will of God prevails. In great contests each party claims to act in accordance with the will of God. Both <u>may</u> be, and one <u>must</u> be wrong...In the present Civil War it is quite possible that God's purpose is something different from the purpose of either party-and yet the human instrumentalities, working just as they do, are of the best adaption to effect His purpose...God wills this contest...'

Washington, D.C. September, 1862

Whatever God allows in your life or mine, he allows for a purpose. This purpose is not always evident and the timing may seem to us very inappropriate from our perspective. However, during these times wisdom, which we are told to continually pray for, will be a key ally in our development and enable us to discern the purposes of God without becoming fearful or anxious. Our ultimate trust in him is what God is after and he knows the best method to achieve this. In the early years of his ministry, the apostle Paul spoke of the hardship they experienced in the province of Asia, and how difficult it was, yet he concludes with the reason as to why it happened *'...this happened that we might not rely on ourselves but on God...'* (2 Corinthians 1:9 NIV).

For me, and no doubt many of you, this reliance on God does not come easily. My up-bringing and education taught me to focus on my abilities to effect change in my life and how to achieve future goals and ambitions. This is not to say that God cannot use human ingenuity, he does, however, our reliance on them could be a hindrance and a stumbling block to the greater things God wants to achieve through, and in us, as our success could be attributed to our own endeavours, rather than leading us to acknowledge the will and favour of God in all of life's circumstances. Our talents and ability to serve God in this life are all gifts from God, including our ability to achieve any form of real success or to gain true wealth and prosperity in this world, free from any form of guilt to richly enjoy and be a blessing to others.

I came across a newspaper heading which really caught my attention because it was so alarming, it read: **MILLIONS MUST WORK FOREVER – Retirement now impossible due to pension crisis.** [Daily Express, 23/10/2012 by Sarah O'Grady] Many people are putting their lives on hold in the hope of enjoying life later. The article warned that this will not be a happy time for many people, in fact the outlook is very bleak due to an aging population and the current economic crisis, even those who do manage to receive a pension will find it to be substantially reduced.

This is not to say that we are not to prepare and make provision for the future. However, it is to the Father's glory that he seeks to establish our dependency upon him and live a life worthy of who we are in Christ, for the current worldly system is flawed in so many ways and full of false hope and deceptions that leads so many individuals into a way of living that is not only futile, but robs them of their identity and true worth.

So many people, myself included, have found themselves in careers and positions of employment that they know they are better than, but feel trapped or unable to change course. The hope our Father offers us is a new, resurrected life, full of potential and good works that are tailor-made to who we are created to be, which is readily available for all his children right now – hope is at hand.

No matter how old you are, your education or background, your opportunity to start again is a prayer away: *For I know the plans I have for you, "declares the Lord, "plans to prosper you and not to harm you, plans to give you hope and a future. Then you will call on me and come and pray to me, and I will listen to you. You will seek me and find me when you seek me with all your heart. I will be found by you," declares the Lord..."* (Jeremiah 29:11-14 NIV).

There will of course be challenges, the Bible tells us that 'many are the afflictions of the righteous', the word of God lets us know the reality of our faith, but with it comes a promise of delivery from each and every challenge. We are a people who, although '...*our citizenship is in heaven*' (Philippians 3:20 NKJV) reside in a fallen world, very much influenced by our adversary. To stand firm and walk in God's will for your life, you must allow yourself time to continually thank God that he has fully equipped you for your assignment and consider you able to handle any conflict because he is with you.

The enemy aims to destroy your faith and trust in the promises of God; God desires your promotion and freedom. Do not lose sight of whom and whose you are. Do not focus on the enemy, focus on God and his power, and allow him to take you through this period of change and growth. We look up and pray and ask the Lord to send us help from his sanctuary as David did, and we trust that his resources will come each day. In the meantime, remember, for all the enemy's attacks and attempts to discourage you, he is a defeated foe. Keep on thanking the Lord for what he has brought you through in the past, and the glorious future awaiting you. We are '...*more than conquerors*' (Romans 8:37 NIV) in Christ Jesus.

Never compromise who you are, when God created you he also blessed you with many unique gifts; these gifts will help you to overcome future challenges. However, to operate proficiently in these gifts will take practice. Musicians know that the more they practice playing an instrument the better they become; likewise athletes have to have strict regimes of training to enable them to compete effectively. The apostle Paul encouraged Timothy to stir up his gifts, to start using them to greater effect for God's glory. Take time to meditate and reflect on your progress in prayer, so as to continually receive guidance and needful encouragement from the Holy Spirit, there are many blessings awaiting you.

Chapter 3

A heavenly apprenticeship awaiting you

Many years ago great artists or craftsmen were not only known for their talents, but under whom they served their apprenticeship. The painter, Raphael, served under the inspirational painter Perugino, who gave him a firm foundation in the craft of painting. Ray Charles and Count Basie were very influential in the life and career of Quincy Jones. It has been said that Clint Eastwood attributes a lot of his success to his parents and his maternal grandmother. There are many more I could mention.

In the Bible we also have this relationship of Godly influence encouraging someone to great levels of achievement, even when that particular individual felt incapable or unable to achieve a task seemingly impossible for them at that time. Joshua was a student of Moses and faithfully fulfilled his duties as Israel's leader when the time came for Moses to depart. Elijah encouraged Elisha to take up his mantle as a prophet; Naomi took Ruth under her wing and gave her advice and instruction on how to live and conduct herself in Israel, which was so anointed, that it resulted in her becoming the great-grandmother of King David.

Today, the universities we attend to obtain the prestigious degrees are in a similar way our badge of accomplishment, having 'served under' Oxford, Cambridge, Stanford etc. These forms of developing ones prestige, talents and acquiring knowledge are good and have led to many great discoveries and inventions. However, not everyone can afford to attend the best educational institutions or pay for private tuition from an expert in their chosen field. We may be fortunate enough to find ourselves in a position where our teacher is a relative, but even this will have its limitations regarding our specific needs, when compared to God's intimate counsel and mentoring strategies for our success in every area of life.

A mentor is said to be 'a person who gives another person help and advice over a period of time and often teaches them how to do their job' (Cambridge Dictionary on-line). I like this definition as it encompasses much of how God works in our own lives during our walk with him. In scripture David a mighty warrior openly, during moments of praise and thanksgiving to God, not only thanks him for protection and vindication from his enemies, but also thanks him that he '...*trains my hand for war, my fingers for battle*' (Psalm 144:1 NIV).

Charles Spurgeon in his commentary on the Psalms, commenting on Psalm 32:8 puts it very succinctly:

'A heavenly training is one of the covenant blessings which adoption seals to us.'

Charles Spurgeon - A Treasury of David

David gives God the glory for his abilities as an outstanding warrior. His training started early in his life as he obediently served the Lord doing what would seem of no profit to a fighting man, tending sheep. However, God in his wisdom used these moments of one-to-one training to teach David how to fight with, and defeat, a lion and a bear. The reason for these lessons I believe became crystal clear to David when he heard about Goliath, and how he was taunting Israel and their God.

I love the Superman films because I see so many parallels to the life of Christ in them. Many film buffs have also commented on this over the years, with each new version bringing for me another aspect related to Christ and the scriptures, such as a father sending his son to earth, who also has a mortal enemy set on his destruction.

In the latest version - Man of Steel, Superman is wrestling with his purpose while trying to find his place in what can only be described as an alien environment. However, this all changes with the arrival of his arch enemy General Zod. In the Man of Steel Publicity Special it was said that Superman '...hadn't quite factored in the idea of being the *saviour of the world* until Zod turns up'.

Likewise, whenever I read the story of David and Goliath I can't help but see David smiling to himself, confident in the knowledge that all his time spent in training with God had been a preparation for this moment, and thanking God for the victory over Goliath. As you read 1 Samuel 17 all seems lost for the nation who feel helpless against the threats of Goliath, this giant champion of the Philistines, as described in verse 11 '*When Saul and all Israel heard these words of the Philistine, they were dismayed and greatly afraid'* (1 Samuel 17:11).

However, the stage is now set to introduce our hero as verse 12 draws our attention to the 'man of faith', trained by God, with two words that introduce light and hope *'Now David...'* (1 Samuel 17:12). David was so confident and courageous through his faith in God, he knew without a shadow of doubt from his experiences with God while protecting the sheep, that God would give him the victory over Goliath. Listen how boldly this young shepherd boy makes his request to King Saul to fight Goliath, and the basis for his confidence, *'Your servant has killed both the lion and the bear...The Lord who delivered me from the paw of the lion and the paw of the bear will deliver me from the hand of this Philistine'* (1 Samuel 17:36-37 NIV).

David learned during his times of training the valuable lessons related to the promise that one day he would be the future King of Israel. Many people are familiar with the story of David and Goliath and see it as just a good 'moral' tale of the small person overcoming a giant obstacle; while conveniently, leaving out the crucial part God plays in the event. Without God there is no victory for David, for you or for me.

In the New Testament this echo continues to ring true in the words of Jesus to all Christians *'...apart from me you can do nothing'* (John 15:5 NIV). Our ability to produce good fruit for the glory of God requires a commitment to being taught, to being open, and to being guided by the Holy Spirit.

The disciples demonstrated this in the New Testament during their open opposition to the religious leaders and teachers of the law, who were confounded by their knowledge and ability to not only address them as equals, but as those with a superior wisdom and knowledge which they were incapable of challenging, '*When they saw the courage of Peter and John and realised that they were unschooled, ordinary men, they were astonished and took note that these men had been with Jesus*' (Acts 4:13 NIV).

The disciples' wisdom was credited not to their 'top schools', because they referred to them as 'unschooled', which they were according to their methods. The disciples had a much greater teacher – Jesus, God himself. The wisdom of his counsel which they openly acknowledged and 'took note' of is power and wisdom available to you as you go about the Lord's business, making his purpose a priority. The Holy Spirit can and will impart to you the knowledge and power necessary pertaining to your ministry that will not only astonish people, but at the same time give God the glory.

To have a mentor for a period of time is one thing, but to have one who walks with you throughout your life, who loves you and has already made provision for every challenge you will face is much better. This is what we all have who are in Christ.

Moreover, we know these principles to be true in everyday family relationships, for year's fathers and mothers have passed on their trade, knowledge and skills to their sons and daughters, a tradition which continues today in many cultures - how much more your heavenly Father.

●●●

Should you still remain unconvinced and in need of further encouragement to trust God, consider this. Research has shown that in the world today and throughout history, the life chances and opportunities that determine what a person becomes in society, predominantly seem to be determined by ones place of birth, family ties and associations. The lack of social mobility in education and employment is an issue many are seeking to address today. Current studies show that most people still remain in the socio-economic conditions that they were brought up in, except for a few. The entrepreneurial route in particular has helped many determined individuals buck this trend. Self-will and determination will always get results, albeit at a price.

The Christian, however, has a more accessible option to achieve true success and prosperity. In Ephesians 2:10 we are told that we are God's '...*workmanship, created in Christ Jesus for good works, which God prepared beforehand that we should walk in them*' (NKJV). Not only did God create a masterpiece when making you, he also drew up a CV tailor made for you, perfectly aligned with the gifts and talents Jesus gave you and the good works which he prepared in advance for you and me to do, works which also come with heavenly blessings and provisions.

F B Myer in his book, Abraham Friend of God, puts God's intention this way:

'A great thinker feels that his end is approaching; he has made grand discoveries, but he has not as yet given them to the world. He selects one of his most promising pupils, and carefully indoctrinates him with his system; he is very severe on any inaccuracies and mistakes; he is very careful to give line on line. Why does he take all this care? For the sake of the young man? Not exclusively for the pupils benefit; but that he may be able to give the world those thoughts which his dying master has confided to his care. The young disciple is blessed that he may pass the blessings on to others'.

p19

At times you may feel that others have a liberty which you do not have, but God knows your future and the valuable lessons you need to learn where he has placed you, in order that your walk with him may be peace and joy, for you are a rich blessing for others that brings glory to God through your life. We never lose with God and, unlike the works guided by greed and selfish ambition, our blessings extend into eternity. Paul had a vision of this when he spoke of a *'crown of righteousness'* awaiting him in heaven. This hope of a great life, here and now, and a glorious future is something that should be very precious to every believer. We have a glorious future in Christ for the taking.

However, God still respects our free will and although we are saved, he will not force our inheritance upon us. The freedom to be who God created us to be speaks to me of true freedom. When

Jesus said '*...I have come that they may have life, and have it to the full.*' (John 10:10 NIV), it helps me to realise that far to often I settle for less than what Jesus came and died for me to have. Challenges will come, for we are told that in this world we will have trouble.

Equally, we may feel fear at what we need to do, finding ourselves in unfamiliar territory as we learn and develop. Doubts will arise as to how God is going to achieve what we know he has spoken to our heart. These are all valid concerns, and in our own strength the outcome is limited. The victory for us is in the fact that Jesus has '*overcome the world*' and leads us from glory to glory, now all things work together for our good.

However, I feel that I must add a word of caution here. As you progress with the Lord you will grow in character, your gifts will begin to make room for you and the blessings of obedience will start to manifest itself in ways that you could not have imagined. You will find that previous desires and ambitions that were difficult for you to obtain are now within easy reach, along with your capabilities to achieve them. Although, these things may not be wrong or bad in themselves, if they divert you from the path God has revealed to you, the detour could be costly.

Many valuable lessons aimed at future challenges would now be wasted or used inappropriately. Staying the course can be difficult, particularly for those who do not understand their calling. These times also raise doubts within us as to whether we are on the right path. During such occasions we need to seek Godly counsel and wait prayerfully until we are sure of the next step. Below is the Serenity Prayer by Reinhold Niebuhr, a full version was given to me recently and I believe at times of doubt and confusion it will help guide you towards God's wisdom when prayed earnestly:

God grant me the serenity
to accept the things I cannot change;

courage to change the things I can;
and wisdom to know the difference.

Living one day at a time;
Enjoying one moment at a time;
Accepting hardship as the pathway to peace;

Taking, as He did, this sinful world
as it is, not as I would have it;
Trusting that He will make all things
right if I surrender to His will;
That I may be reasonably happy in this life
and supremely happy with Him
Forever in the next.
Amen

Reinhold Niebuhr in 1943

Chapter 4

You cannot serve both God and Mammon (wealth)

There are many things in life which cause us problems, but by far one of the greatest is the fear of not having enough money. Our society today relies on it so much that if something cannot be done or achieved, lack of money is usually seen as the cause. However, it would be equally unrealistic in most societies to attempt to live these days without money. I know that there are some who attempt to break free from a reliance on money by becoming self-sufficient, but for the vast majority this is impractical.

From my understanding of the Bible, God is not against wealth, in Deuteronomy 8:18 (NIV) it says to '...*remember the Lord your God, for it is He who gives you the ability to produce wealth*'. John D. Rockefeller, one of the richest men who ever lived, unashamedly stated that 'God gave me money' and by his own account spoke of having ways of making money that he hadn't even explored.

So what should our view be concerning money and wealth, and are there any valuable lessons from scripture to be learnt for our benefit? I think there is. I believe that when Jesus used Peter's boat to launch out into the deep, making such a catch that Peter needed help to carry the fish ashore (Luke 5:1-7), he was giving us an insight into his authority over wealth. Here we have in the word of God a picture of the abundance of heaven and sure knowledge of God's ability to provide, compared to the high price paid by so many to acquire worldly wealth and the self-effort, along with the compromises so often necessary to achieve this apart from God.

This picture can be superimposed onto any of life's circumstances. Like Peter, our part is to trust, obey and to receive the abundance, without fear, regret or harm to ourselves or loved ones.

I often use mental pictures to help me grasp a biblical truth. In this case I see money as one of Satan's henchmen who is in direct opposition to God and his children. Os Guinness mentions in his book The Call (p139-140), the negative influence money can have in our daily lives:

> *'The problem is that money can assume an inordinate place in our lives until it becomes a personal, spiritual, god-like force that rules us – Mammon.'*

This 'spiritual henchman' I picture as deliberately trying to undermine our reliance and trust on God's provision, and is always seeking to frustrate our hope and ultimately our belief in God.

It does this by bombarding us with negative thoughts like, 'you need me', or 'only I can get you what you desire', 'if you have me you are free to do what you like' or 'your life will be fine, then they will respect you'. These and many other comments, I am sure you can add a few of your own, have one aim in mind and that is to undermine our belief in the authority and promises of scripture, the genuine wealth and power available to us on a daily basis, thereby frustrating our walk of faith and reliance on God, which leads to real freedom.

Jesus said that we are to *'...seek first his kingdom...'* (Matthew 6:33 NIV). If we make this a priority in our lives all the other things which the Father knows we have need of and that the world runs after, will automatically be given to us. Moreover, in Psalm 37:4 we are told to *'Delight yourself also in the Lord, and He shall give you the desires of your heart'*. (NKJV) The Amplified Bible says 'secret desires', things only known by God, but which he wants you to know and also enjoy through your privilege to fellowship with him.

This is not an instruction to 'down tools' and drop all our existing commitments and responsibilities. This is not about getting 'religious'. It is about having a heart attitude in which God's priorities become our priorities. That is when we are putting the kingdom of God first. The promise we have from scripture is that when we do this we are truly living the abundant life Jesus wants us to receive, *'I am come that they might have life, and that they might have it more abundantly'* (John 10:10 KJV).

So, where do we start? First, we all have to ask ourselves this question - am I serving money or is money serving me? The Greek word used for 'serve' here is douleuo and is referred to in Vine's Dictionary as bondage – to serve as a slave. The apostle Paul uses a similar term in the positive sense when he referred to himself in Romans 1:1 as a servant (doulos) of Christ Jesus. The Bible promises us that *'...God shall supply all your need according to his riches in glory by Christ Jesus'* (Philippians 4:19 KJV). Our part is to believe.

We serve a good God who has not only committed himself to supplying all our needs, but who also wants to bless us with the desires of our heart, known and unknown. We are blessed here and now, and the time to taste and see that the Lord is good should not be wasted. In eternity to come we will be continually reliant on the goodness and love of God. The same God, who has made provision for you and me in the future, has also made provision for us now. His love for us is an everlasting love that has never and will never diminish in its intensity.

Before I go any further I am not telling you to be irresponsible with money, on the contrary we are to be wise stewards. What I want you to focus on are the areas in your life where you have through fear of loss, neglected others or yourself of something they or you needed.

Part of the money henchman's role is to make us fearful to spend for fear of not having enough later on. I know from my own experiences that when I had very little money, my tendency was to be constantly thinking of how not to spend too much, opting to do without and always wondering how the next bill was going to be paid, concerned that I would not have enough to see me through until I would get paid at the end of the month.

If such a situation goes on for a long time, we can become a people who are in a constant state of anxiety about our finances, to the point that even if we do find ourselves with a little extra cash, we think that it should not be spent as we are bound to need it later. Now, in some cases this may well be true, but God does not want his children to live like this. These feelings are not limited to people who are struggling financially, many wealthy people also experience these feelings. Money is a cruel and ruthless master that has led many people to act and behave in ways that they would never have imaged or believed possible, ways that have destroyed the integrity, character and reputation of many, overnight.

When we embrace our calling and seek to live for God, he will take care of all of our needs and if we are blessed financially there is no guilt attached to it. Paul poses a rhetorical question in 1 Corinthians 9:7, 'W*ho serves as a soldier at his own expense?*' (NIV) When we serve Christ, he takes care of our provision. Psalm 23:1 also tells us that the Lord is our Shepherd and we shall not be in want. There are many more verses that make these promises, something we can hold onto in prayer without fear. By doing so, we send Satan's money henchman packing and open up the door to God's store house of provision by faith, which will never fail. Like a stream of blessings, your daily needs will be supplied.

To enable this to become a regular practice we must first apply the words of Jesus from the Gospel of Matthew (6:34) where he says to '*...not worry about tomorrow, for tomorrow will worry about itself.*' (NIV) We must become a people who LIVE each day - not just survive, who enjoy what we have NOW. The worries tend to come quickly when we start to look too far ahead or compare ourselves and what we have to someone else. The more we start to look ahead about how God will provide in the future, the darker it seems and Satan's money henchman knows how to play on our inner fears.

The Bible says that God will, *'...keep him in perfect peace...'* (Isaiah 26:3 NKJV), whose mind is focused on him. Don't give the enemy any of your time; he is an attention seeker who has no authority in your life. Rather, praise God and believe the truth you have available to you revealed in scripture. Take time to thank God for all he is doing in your life and the daily mercies already received, seen and unseen. When we do this it shows that we are mature children, who at times may stumble and fall. But God knows our hearts because we speak and apply the truth as ones who are building their houses on a sure foundation that cannot fail - his Word.

The word of God reassures us that '...*the Lord watches over the way of the righteous...*' (Psalm 1:6 NIV), we, who have been redeemed by the blood of Christ, are declared righteous by God and therefore have every reason to live in hope, even when tempted to doubt or feel fearful. This 'watching' is not a detached, passive observance from a distance; this is genuine fellowship between God and his children, a loving relationship more intimate and passionate than anything we could ever experience with our family members or dearest friends.

One of my favourite films is The Karate Kid. In the first film Daniel Larusso, the young hero, seems to be wasting his time washing and waxing cars, when he was hoping to be taught how to fight using Karate against a gang of bullies. The phrase 'wax on, wax off' is very familiar to many of my generation. However, there was a hidden lesson being taught in these instructions from his elderly and wise teacher, Mr Miyagi, for all the time he was spending just waxing cars in the specific manner shown to him by his mentor, he was developing basic skills and responses, vital for Karate, skills he would have to call upon instinctively in the competitive fighting challenges he was about to face. What appeared endlessly boring and monotonous to him would become the very foundation and means of his success.

Mr Miyagi knew Daniel, his weaknesses, what lay ahead and had to prepare him to meet them successfully, so that when faced with challenges and pressure so great as to momentarily cause confusion, Daniel would be able to rely on techniques so established within him, that his fighting reactions would be automatic. This unorthodox training method seemed confusing to Daniel at first, but he did see the ultimate benefit of Mr Miyagi's wisdom, even though the exercise initially seemed pointless and totally unrelated to what he thought was important.

God's ways likewise are not our ways and he will tailor our training based on our future challenges. This is where knowledge of your calling and natural abilities given by God are crucial as, *'A man's gift makes room for him...'* (Proverbs 18:16, NASB). In many instances the challenges that we face will seem insurmountable, unless we learn to recognise the valuable lessons the Holy Spirit is trying to teach us and become good students in order to be fruitful servants. A note of caution, as Christians, we can achieve a great deal outside of this relationship, through our own will and determination; however, as children of God our consciences will never truly be at rest and we should give heed to such warning signals, always remembering that God's plan for our lives is perfect, *'For I know the plans I have for you, declares the Lord, plans to prosper you and not to harm you, plans to give you hope and a future'* (Jeremiah 29:11 NIV).

For example, an individual who knows God and more importantly is known by God, having spent quality time with God, listening to Godly counsel and seeking to be obedient to their calling and his will, may have felt called to be a plumber and the Lord has gifted that individual with everything necessary for that calling. However, to develop those skills and in a way that will draw out that gifting, the prospective plumber may start to experience leaking pipes. Now, I am not saying God brings bad things into our lives, when he works it is always done in love and with foreknowledge.

An individual, who has no knowledge of his calling would view this as a major problem that could prove expensive, as well as being a cause of frustration, even fear, as to what damage may be caused to his home. However, the prospective plumber will see the leaking pipes from a different perspective. Rather than a problem to be feared, for him this situation becomes an ideal opportunity to walk in faith, believe God and operate as an over-comer. He will instinctively use what God has been teaching him or placed at his disposal to resolve the problem, and by faith, repair those leaking pipes.

The victory will be his to enjoy, the reward of faith put into practice, the faithfulness of God will help him to grow to a point where nothing will intimidate him, why? because God is with him *'Truly I tell you,, if you have faith as small as a mustard seed, you can say to this mountain, 'Move...' and it will move.'* (Matthew 17:20 NIV).

In this victorious spirit we persevere, mistakes will inevitably be made as we learn to put into practice the truths revealed to us, but we carry on believing God, while simultaneously casting down all imaginations that will attempt to discourage us from trusting in the authority and knowledge of God. This is truly being released from the limitations and fears of this world to flourish for the kingdom of God and part of the abundant, joyful life Jesus spoke of us being able to enjoy now on earth in John 10:10, stated in the Amplified Bible as life – to the full, till it overflows.

In the final showdown in the Karate Kid, Mr Miyagi knew Daniel had now learnt what it took to gain the victory and although Daniel was hurt during the fighting competitions, his injuries did not prevent him from ultimately defeating all challengers. The Lord himself becomes personally involved with our challenges, watching over us in order to ensure we too fight the good fight. The apostle Paul mentions in Romans 8:37, through his guidance and strength we cannot lose and will become more than conquerors in Christ.

If you are unsure about what God created and gifted you to do, spend some quiet time in prayer asking him, he wants you to know, but be open to the answer, it may not be what you expect! You have nothing to fear, but everything to gain in praying and seeking God's will, it is for us as Christians a safe place of rest and genuine fellowship with our heavenly Father. Below are a few words to help you get started in your prayer:

Heavenly Father, I thank you that I am fearfully and wonderfully made and that you have a specific plan and purpose for my life. Open my heart and mind to hear your voice and be obedient in what you have called me to do. Teach me to use the gifts and talents you have blessed me with, in a way that is pleasing to you and glorifies your name. I ask this Father in the name of your Son, my Lord and Saviour, Jesus Christ. Amen

Our free will can now come into agreement with God, in a way that we know is pleasing to God. The individual called to be a plumber can now by faith seek to progress in his calling by building up a library of books on plumbing, even exploring the possibilities of starting his own business:

'...Understand that those areas in which our wills are *united* bring into play cosmic forces, and there is literally no limit to what can be achieved...'

Fr John Woolley, I AM WITH YOU, p116

When the prospective plumber asks for such things in prayer, he can now pray confidently knowing that he is not asking amiss and because there is a growing relationship with God, delay, even refusal and correction are received in a way that does not produce anxiety or resentment, but confidence that God will work things out to his advantage, at the right time. The result is peace for the believer, not striving like the pagan, for '...*those who seek the Lord lack no good thing.*

Building your Foundation: Two types of builders - the wise and foolish

In the parable of The Wise and Foolish Builders (Luke 6:47-49), we see the benefits of being a follower of Christ. Not just as one who listens, but one who is actively seeking to put into practice what is heard. The key element of this beautiful parable is the effect our obedience has on the foundation of our lives. Notice, that the time to put the words of God into practice is not when the storm comes, by then it is too late, the time is now, when you know the truth. Christ is our rock and can guide us to build a strong foundation to anchor us through any situation, whether it be financial or marital problems, family matters or work commitments. God knows you and knows what is best for you.

Even though we know this to be true, it is not as easy as it seems to walk through, I would be amiss if I were to give you that impression. The reality is that to be obedient will require disciplined self sacrifice and allowing God's will to take precedence over yours, in many cases in spite of your feelings and misgivings. The end result of obedience however, will always be in our favour, and our understanding that God is for us and not against us will inevitably lead us to greater trust in the future.

When first planted the palm tree can take up to six years just to form its roots, during which time above ground it looks as if nothing is happening. After this period however, once a firm 'foundation' has been established it grows rapidly, reaching up to ninety feet tall in some cases. The tree now can bend and endure many severe storms without breaking. In addition to this it is also rich in fruit and its leaves have many uses that are of benefit to us today.

Many people, in ignorance might have looked at the palm tree during those first six years after it was planted and said 'this plant is dead and will never grow or produce anything'. Some people close to you may be coming to similar erroneous conclusions about some aspects of your life where you are seeking to be obedient to God, because time has gone by with seemingly little results. Don't worry, God has declared you righteous and he is faithful, the work which he has begun in you, he is more than able to complete. Stand firm and 'rest on the rock', your time will come!

However, where there is revelation there is also accountability. Rebellion against God – not doing what you know to be his will or not being patient always has consequences and one not necessarily of our choosing. This is not always evident when we first start to rebel, on the contrary, in many cases the illusion is one of success, but it is an illusion, when viewed in the light of eternity and the final judgement.

This is not to say that we will never make mistakes or feel apprehension. With the best will in the world, seeking to do the right thing and be obedient, we may still get it wrong. However, God's grace is consistently with us to enable us to continue, not as failures, but as dearly loved children who are learning the family business.

When a family adopts a 'troubled child', they are normally well briefed beforehand about the child's history, including personal struggles and emotional issues. The adopting parents agree to have the child with this full knowledge in the hope that the new environment they will offer, one of love and care, will enable that child to grow up healthy and approach life differently, free from past hurts and limitations.

As children of God, brought into this glorious relationship by the sacrifice of Christ, we are adopted into God's family. A family devoted to our care and provision that loves us regardless of our failings and always has our best interest at heart. We are all struggling with something and as long as we are in these earthly bodies we always will be, the Bible says that '...*each one is tempted when he is drawn away by his own desires and enticed.*' (James 1:14, NKJV). Even though we do struggle, we as Christians have reason for rejoicing, especially in the storms of life, Jesus says in John 10:29 ' *My Father, who has given them to me, is greater than all; no-one can snatch them out of my Father's hand.*' (NKJV). We have a glorious inheritance.

Where the adoptive parents are limited, insofar as they love their newly adopted child, they cannot physically make that child a part of their family. God can, when we received Christ as our Lord and Saviour, we also received the Spirit of Christ, the first fruits of our inheritance, a deposit of things to come. From this perspective we move forward as life's over-comers, from glory to glory.

Chapter 5

Waiting on God

In the Christian life, one of the most challenging things to do is to wait patiently. This act goes against many of our human faculties, or should I say frailties. When we know that God, in a very real sense, has given us a particular promise regarding a certain situation; the initial joy can gradually start to wane the longer we wait. Our grip seems to become weaker, until sentiments of doubt, rather than faith, are uppermost in our heart.

Was this not the case with Abraham? After God had appeared to him and said *"To your offspring I will give this land"* (Genesis 12:7 NIV), you can imagine Abraham's joy. The journey and his obedience was to be rewarded with a land of his own, something that he would be able to pass on to his children. However, as the time went on this joy is not evident in his answer to God in a future divine visitation, *'"Sovereign Lord, what can you give me since I remain childless..."'* (Genesis 15:2 NIV). When is your promise to me going to come about is what Abraham was really asking.

Sometimes we look at the outward circumstances and reason that God cannot fulfil what he has led us to believe, the task is too great, I know I do. However, to look at things from our perspective is only viewing things through our limited comprehension of the facts and God's power. God sees the whole picture. He lets us know through these valuable times of testing involving setbacks and delays, that his ways are not our ways, for he says in Isaiah 55:8 *"...my thoughts are not your thoughts, neither are your ways my ways..."* (KJV).

Although, in our hearts we know this to be true, it only seems to make the delay even more confusing, why doesn't he act? So like the Psalmist in Psalm 77:7-8, we start to say *'...Will he never show his favour again? Has his unfailing love vanished forever? Has his promise failed for all time?* (NIV). These and many other questions we ask until, in the end, we assume that we must have done something wrong and conclude that God has overlooked us.

Moreover, on this issue David also experienced similar circumstances in his attacks from King Saul. Although strong in faith and a man, scripture says, '...after God own heart', the Bible tells us in his despair with the continued and relentless attacks against him due to Saul's jealousy, David thought to himself, *"One of these days I will be destroyed by the hand of Saul."* (1 Sam 27:1 NIV). In both cases God's word remained true, Abraham received his promised son Isaac, along with other children and David was not destroyed by the hand of Saul, but as his anointing prophesied, became King of Israel.

These and many other examples from scripture are meant to teach us something, but what exactly? Well, what we have in these incidences are pictures of the battle ground of faith, where God poses his own questions such as that found in Isaiah 49:15 *'"Can a mother forget the baby at her breast...though she may forget, I will not forget you!"'* (NIV). This is a very reassuring verse in scripture regarding our relationship with God. My mother would tell me how difficult it was for her to speak and relate to her elderly mother - my grandmother, who developed Dementia as she got older. There were times when she would not even recognise my mother at all - asking her who she was. This was painful for my mother to experience.

Our relationship with God cannot be broken in any way *'...neither death nor life...neither present nor the future...will be able to separate us from the love of God that is in Christ Jesus our Lord'* (Romans 8:38-39 NIV), his love and understanding comes from a perfect knowledge of who we are. When we are tempted to feel abandoned by man and forgotten by friends and family, whether through ill health or deliberately, we can always rely on our heavenly Father, who not only loves us, but remembers how we blessed his heart when we accepted the gift of his son Jesus.

His covenant promise to always do us good now holds true for every born again believer, a covenant that will never be broken, not in this life or eternity to come. Waiting can be done joyfully if we see the delay as being spiritually expedient. God can use these periods to our advantage and profit to give us a greater understanding and trust in his character and faithfulness to us.

In his book Shadow Warriors, Tom Clancy, talks about the training of elite, Special Forces soldiers who are preselected and prepared for special military combat in a hostile environment. They have to undergo a form of sensory deprivation, as part of their training regime. They at times can be left in a particular location without knowing for how long and have to use their military skills to survive, while living with the native population. They are given instructions to perform certain tasks without any details as to how or when to complete them, or whether they have done them correctly or not:

> '...like all soldiers Special Forces men work under a chain of command, but unlike the others they may not always have direct or even regular communication with their superiors. That means that at times they need to act on their own, which means they inevitably make decisions on their own, though based, it is hoped, on a clear understanding of their commanders and their nations intent.'
>
> Tom Clancy - Shadow Warriors

Why do they have to go through this as part of their training? As a soldier you need to know without a shadow of doubt that you are part of a unit that is ready to support you at any time. However, the need for constant approval can be a hindrance because some campaigns are lengthy and if you are someone who needs to be constantly affirmed, your ability to stay focused when no one is patting you on the back will be compromised. The successful soldier is the one who remains focused, completing the tasks, knowing that they are not abandoned.

On completing this training, the ones who stayed the course are of great value to their commanding officers and fellow soldiers, as they can be relied upon to complete tasks even if no-one is cheering them on or forcing them to do it. They can be trusted with more responsibilities and are able to teach others from their own experiences. They have a lot more freedom as a result and the ability to cope in diverse situations, where others would be fearful.

Now don't get me wrong, it is nice to be encouraged and have popular support in our endeavours. However, the reality for the Christian is that if we are to be obedient to the truth as revealed in scripture, we will find that, for the most part, we are in direct opposition to the views of society. We may be falsely accused and in some cases persecuted. To persevere without compromise we will have to know without any uncertainty, regardless of all outward circumstances to the contrary, that God is faithful and can be trusted.

After the crucifixion and resurrection of Jesus, prior to his ascension there was much confusion amongst the disciples, not to mention apprehension as to what the future may hold. During this time Jesus would appear to his disciples one minute and then vanish, before appearing again at some unknown time or place. Why was he doing this? We are given the answer by Jesus in his reply to Thomas *'Because you have seen me, you have believed; blessed are those who have not seen and yet have believed'* (John 20:29 NIV).

He wanted their faith to be founded on knowing that whether they saw him or not, he was always with them.

Similarly, in the Old Testament many of God's servants had to learn this lesson, including Abraham, who the Bible refers to as the friend of God. He had some great experiences with God, but equally, there were many long years in between where God was silent. Like us, his faith had to be built on a sure foundation.

F.B Meyer in his book Abraham Friend of God explains the reason as to why we experience such delays and how to accept them as a path to maturity:

'...when the child of God has lost these bright visitations for long and sad intervals – if, so far as can be ascertained, there is no sense of condemnation on the heart for known unfaithfulness – then it must be believed that they are withheld, not in consequence of palpable sin, but to test the inner life, and to teach the necessity of basing it on faith, rather than feelings however gladsome, or experiences however divine.'

p80

As Christians, if we are to advance successfully in the kingdom of heaven, we will need to remember that we are *'in this world, but not of it'*. Times of testing will come, not to break us, but to free us from our fears and prepare us for useful service as children of God. In Hebrews 12:7 we are told to *'Endure hardship as discipline...'* (NIV). However, this is not the end of the story, there is a good reason, for it *'...produces a harvest of righteousness and peace for those who have been trained by it'* (Hebrews 12:11 NIV).

Having already declared all born-again believers righteous, our God who establishes the end from the beginning and calls those things that are not as though they are, begins a great work in us and he who has begun this work is faithful to complete it. Your life is not subject to chance or circumstance; it is directed and established by your heavenly Father. So upon this realisation what is our next step to be?

Well, back to Romans 8 where Paul concludes and affirms our position by saying that *'In all these things we are more than conquerors through Him who loved us'*. If we can learn to use this time to develop some key biblical truths in our lives, we would be much more able to handle whatever comes against us in the future. Patience is a valuable fruit of the Spirit, which can be attributed to those who have been called to endure times of hardship. I believe that an alternative perspective is always helpful when seeking to explain such an important principle. We all look forward to Christmas (well most of us), especially as children, but if a child refused to enjoy the rest of the year and in February was sad and withdrawn, refusing to be happy until Christmas came around again, this I am sure would cause some concern.

An intense focus on anything can cause an unnatural imbalance in our daily lives. This is how sin came into the world in the first place, by Adam and Eve focusing on the one tree God said to stay away from. Can you imagine what the other trees in the Garden of Eden were like? You only have to look at nature, the beautiful flowers, trees and variety of colours to know that God would have made available to them a fabulous range of other trees for them to explore and enjoy in the garden.

While we are waiting on God where he has placed us, we should explore the 'other trees', so-to-speak, in our particular garden, that God has made readily available at this moment in our lives. Especially those related to our ministry. This is a time to stir up the gifts and talents God has richly blessed us with for use in the future.

Until now you may have possibly focussed on what you do not have, what I would like to do is to draw your attention to what you do have access to. When God put Adam in the Garden of Eden, he gave him many trees to eat from and in a manner of speaking, we also in our own lives at present have many good things we could be doing while waiting upon the promise.

This is not as haphazard an exercise as you may think. It is aimed at you specifically. It starts with asking God about your own ministry, whether that be as a doctor, scientist, nurse, lawyer, plumber, secretary, businessperson, carer, entrepreneur, whatever your ministry is, that's your garden! Let me explain, if for example you are called to be a plumber and God has promised to bless you greatly, while waiting, find out what you would need to start your business, look at prime sites where you would like to be based, find out costs etc., and make these things part of your prayer life.

God knows exactly where you are and he will be with you, guiding you every step of the way. Proverbs 16:3 says, *'Commit your works to the Lord, and your thoughts will be established'* (NKJV). It might not work out exactly as you might have imagined, but by committing your actions prayerfully and walking in hope, you will be delighting yourself in the Lord.

From a worldly perspective we can surely appreciate someone who not only listens to what we say, but chooses to become part of a good cause without being forced. As you start to sense God's guidance, you will realise that his promise to never leave us or forsake us is true. This will be a comforting truth that will not only make your waiting bearable, but productive.

Of course, this assumes you know what your ministry is. If you do not, then I would suggest you focus your prayers first to find out exactly what God has created and gifted you to do. The bible tells us in Ephesians 2:10 *'For we are His workmanship, created in Christ Jesus for good works, which God prepared beforehand that we should walk in them'* (NKJV).

No matter where you are, how old you may be, or whatever your circumstances, God can and will use you if you will let him. Many of your gifts and talents, including those yet to be developed are meant to compliment your ministry. By getting on-board with God's programme, you will find him more than willing to guide you, as you, in a very practical sense use your time to explore the 'other trees' in your garden.

The next thing to do as your walk with God begins to increase your faith, making you less anxious, is to pray for someone else. Intercession is power in practice; your prayers are powerful weapons. These actions help us to become more and more transformed into the image of Christ. Jesus said, *'Learn of me'* and also made it clear that he *'Must be about his Father's business'*.

Whenever he could, Jesus got up early and took time aside to go and pray. If the Son of God needed to do this, guess what, we do too! Even on the cross Jesus was interceding when he said *'Father, forgive them, for they know not what they do'*. When we look at our family, friends, community, our government and make them part of our prayers, we show a level of maturity, which I believe God really does appreciate.

During this time we should also find something to give thanks for. This may not always be as easy as it sounds, I know, but give it a try. Once you start you will see how much God has already blessed you. It could be giving thanks for your loved ones, friends, food, clothing, access to a doctor, a telephone, anything good, because we are told '...*all good gifts come from God*' and if you still can't think of anything after that, thank him for enabling me to write this book!

Psalm 100:4 says '*Enter His gates with thanksgiving and His courts with praise*' (NIV). I believe that once you start to see how God has already blessed you the result is inevitably to want to praise him. This stage is what I call 'changing the record'. Previously your thoughts may have primarily been focussed on what you did not have, now you enter into his light and you too have light, as it says in Psalm 36:9 '...*in your light we see light*' (NIV).

The promise remains, but now as your fellowship grows the perspective is balanced and you start to enjoy each day while 'waiting for Christmas' (as the previous analogy), enjoying the 'garden' and developing your ministry. This is when the Christian life really becomes fun. Psalm 100 also says that '....*we are the sheep of His pasture*'. Whatever God will have you do, he will also provide what you need while establishing you, for our Lord is the 'Good Shepherd'.

Finally, the thing I would like to mention is the importance of doing something purely because it makes you laugh, something enjoyable. The Bible says the *'...joy of the Lord is our strength'*. It is very easy to become dour, selfish and insular when we do not have what we have set our hearts on, postponing our happiness to a later date, but all the while being a bad advert for the faith. Make time to have fun with family, friends, the TV guide, whatever you enjoy, do it! You will sleep better and feel better. If you can't think of anything then ask the Lord in your prayer time and explore the 'garden'. Now and then you will feel down and start to worry, but remember to get back on track once you are able.

Chapter 6

Being released is different from escaping

When we experience prolonged periods of trials and hardship, it is perfectly natural to want to be free from these burdens. Many a time, in our Christian walk, we will be utterly confused by how God is bringing his plan about in our lives. We want to do what's right and as far as we are aware, although not perfect, we are seeking to be obedient. So why are things not only so difficult now, but seem to be getting worse?

This wrestling in our heart even starts to question the wisdom of God for leading us down, what appears to be a dead end. Prayer and worship at these times can also become increasingly difficult. How should we handle such times and what valuable lessons can we learn? Moreover, what insights can be gained that will help us to manage more effectively the future challenges, which will inevitably come to anyone seeking to mature their faith?

Since becoming a Christian, I have had many situations in which I have felt totally overwhelmed and confused. Fear as to how I was going to cope also started to challenge my faith. I wanted to find a quick fix, a way out to escape the problem because of the way it was making me feel. I looked around at other believers and concluded none of them were going through what I was going through, something is wrong, why am I being treated so unfairly?

In the midst of my confusion, I still felt that God was trying to teach me something, what exactly I didn't know, but his words of comfort never left me, although I found them hard to believe at such times. Then I began to look at the life of Joseph and how he was mistreated, falsely accused and sent to jail. He too felt that he should not be in prison, and even asked Pharaoh's cupbearer after interpreting his dream to, '*...mention me to Pharaoh and get me out of this prison...*' (Gen 40:14 NIV).

I can totally sympathise with Joseph, after being falsely accused and held in prison for so many years, I too would have wanted to get out as soon as possible. However, Joseph's own response after his release to his brothers, who were fearful that Joseph would take revenge for their actions against him, was very telling. Released from prison and now in the position of authority (Prime Minister of Egypt), which God had shown him previously in two distinct dreams, Joseph saw the bigger picture and was able to say, '*You intended to harm me, but God intended it for good to accomplish what is now being done, the saving of many lives*' (Genesis 50:20 NIV).

Joseph did not deny the intentions of his brothers to harm him, but in retrospect recognised that God was working all the time with a specific plan and purpose in mind, not just for his life, but to benefit the lives of many others. We also are chosen by God for a specific plan and purpose which, once trained, we are released into in order to be a blessing in the lives of others.

The attitude and expectation of someone who has been released is totally different to an escapee. The mindset of a fugitive is constantly uneasy, always anxious that what they fear will come upon them at some unexpected moment. The released individual on the other hand has no such fear. The Bible tells us that, '... *if the Son sets you free, you will be free indeed*' (John 8:36 NIV). Therefore, as Christians, we are assured that whatever we are going through, God is working on our behalf and will always work the situation for good, in spite of our doubts.

A key to understanding and appreciating how God is working in our lives at present is to have and maintain an effectual prayer life and an attitude of thankfulness.

Throughout this book you will hear me mention the importance of prayer. I would like to spend a little time just explaining what this means to me and hopefully it will help you. When I look at my prayer life now, compared to when I first became a Christian, there is no comparison. My understanding of prayer has also changed in a way that enables me to be more relaxed. I was anxious in prayer, not sure what to expect. However, through my own persistence, ignorance and misunderstanding, I continued to seek God in the best way I knew how to.

I grew up in an era when it was considered rude to answer or talk back to your parents; you did as you were told. So for me, one of the most difficult lessons I had to learn regarding my prayer life was that it is a conversation where I not only listened, but was invited to speak, ask for things and even question God.

This got me thinking about how I relate to others and how they communicate with me.   The way I converse with my wife is different to how I converse with my daughters and I conversed differently with my daughters when they were two years old compared to them now, as adults. Likewise, our communication with friends and family vary immensely according to the level of intimacy, maturity and knowledge of each other.

The conversation I have with members of my family will also vary depending on what is going on in their lives. Likewise, when we listen and pray to God during our quiet time, we enter into a deep level of intimacy that enables us not only to speak to God, but hear what is on his heart regarding our current circumstances, as well as future plans. This level of communication is important because the trials and tests we face are unique to us, although we can learn from others who have gone through similar situations.

Listening to God is the most important aspect of a successful walk of faith and will release perpetual blessings if what is heard is combined with faith and converted into trusting obedience. Moreover, by doing this we can ask for things expecting an answer because we are confident based on what God has revealed previously. When we embrace what God is saying and actively embrace what he has for us, then we will ask according to his will.

To be released into your prayer life, is to pray to God and relate to him in a way that speaks to your purpose in life and the inheritance he has allotted to you. Spending time alone with your heavenly Father is by no means a selfish act, on the contrary, it is a blessing to you and those around you. Jesus regularly took time from all the demands of the people to be alone with the Father.

We also need to practice this in order to make an impact in this world for the Father's glory.

One of the benefits of prayer is getting to know God more intimately and being able to accept delay, times of doubt and confusion more readily, based on a deeper relationship and knowledge of God's love for us personally. Without this we will always have some doubts as to why we are led down certain paths and be tempted to feel abandoned by God. This time alone with God also helps us to realise that we have unique God given gifts and talents that he wants to reveal and develop in a way that produces good fruit in our and others lives - fruit that will last.

Because of your time alone with God, delayed answer to prayer, even loss will produce an acceptance which for others will be difficult, if not impossible to handle. Although trials, temptations and doubts will come, we will now be able to enter more fully into the presence of God boldly and proclaim like David, *'Hear a just cause, O Lord, give heed to my cry; give ear to my prayer, which does not come from deceitful lips'* (Psalm 17:1 NASB).

Being in his presence is so empowering that it will produce a sense of peace and knowing that our prayers will be answered. This level of intimacy is, what I believe God wants to have with all of his children, because not only does it produce in us the confidence to ask with expectant hearts, it frees us from the fear of the enemy and all those who would seek to frustrate God's plan for our lives.

You cannot continually fellowship with God without realising how powerful and glorious he is in every aspect of his character, and how deep his love is for us. This sets us free, not only to pursue our calling with confidence, but even setbacks and discipline, which we all receive, will be accepted in love and understanding. When we truly understand that God is for us and not against us, we have been set free from fear, doubt, anxiety or anything that would seek to undermine his authority in our heart and mind.

When Jesus spoke to the Samaritan woman at Jacob's Well, he made it quite clear that he knew about her life *'"You are right when you say you have no husband. The fact is, you have had five husbands, and the man you now have is not your husband..."'* (John 4:17-18 NIV). However, given the fact that such behaviour was frowned upon and made her an outcast, her reaction was amazing. This women was so encouraged by her conversation with Jesus that she actually boasted about her conversation with him to others, *'"...He told me everything I ever did"'* (John 4:39 NIV).

This woman was released. There was something about the way Jesus spoke to her that was so powerful, the Bible says that many Samaritans believed in Jesus because of her testimony. In spite of what the people in this woman's community might have felt about her, through her conversation with Jesus she was set free. So much so that she could not contain herself and wanted others to experience and share her joy.

When we fellowship with the Lord based on who he says we are - righteous and free from condemnation, we too can experience this joy and peace. We frustrate this process however, by our own reluctance to believe that God has truly forgiven us. The evidence of sin still remains and we are constantly reminded that our flesh wars against our spirit. However, like the Samaritan woman at

Jacob's Well, it is our duty to put a greater emphasis on what God says to and about us, than the opinions of others.

Therefore, now when I am doing his will, I do it as one released from the world's view of success. Some days, in obedience to God, it may seem as if I have achieved very little. However, scripture tells us that *'As the heavens are higher than the earth, so are my ways higher than your ways and my thoughts than your thoughts'* (Isaiah 55:9 NIV). During testing times we will all struggle to maintain a firm faith that God can work the situation for good. From a natural perspective it may even seem impossible. Everyday, we will have to quash doubts about God, not only when things look bleak, but when someone else is blessed with what we had hoped for.

God is never complacent during our difficult times. The enemy will try to make us feel as if we have been abandoned and left to find our own solutions. These lies are aimed at producing fear within us, in order to remove our trust and confidence in God and get us to find an alternative solution based on our own efforts. Although tempting, this would be a mistake, because whatever lesson the Lord may be trying to teach us would be lost and hinder our ability to successfully tackle the future challenges the Lord knows we will face.

We all have things going on in our lives that are necessary and need prioritising; these things are not bad or evil in themselves. However, when they develop into forming fearful or anxious thoughts in us, we should heed Jesus' words to Martha when she spoke to him about Mary, her sister, who was not helping her, but rather sitting at Jesus' feet and listening to what he was saying,

'"Martha, Martha,…you are worried and upset about many things, but only one thing is needed. Mary has chosen what is better…"' (Luke 10:41-42 NIV).

It is not that Jesus was indifferent to Martha's concerns, he loved both Martha and Mary, but he knew that with him being present Martha had no need to entertain anything that would rob her of her peace. We also have this promise of God's continual presence and when in times of confusion, we too can sit knowing that he is with us and expect guidance when we hand over our concerns and commit our plans to him. As citizens of heaven we now have this right as a privilege.

Our prayer time should also include confirmation that we are in and doing the will of God, for as we make his priority our main concern, he takes care of providing everything we need, not just for us, but for our family as well, our Lord is the Good Shepherd *'He tends his flock like a shepherd: He gathers the lambs in his arms and carries them close to his heart; he gently leads those that have young'* (Isaiah 40:11 NIV). This assurance is important, as it will also help us to confront challenges and criticisms with great boldness and confidence.

A word of warning, pride, envy, jealousy and fear has led many to view another person's ministry as preferable to their own. They have stumbled in several ways. They have either rejected what God has called them to do through fear or a general dislike or reluctance to embrace their God given ministry, or they have chosen their own way and expect God to come on board with their plans. God is gracious and merciful and will always seek to encourage us to do what is right, but he is under no obligation to support what he has not called us to do. However, because of his goodness he will very often act in such a way that will seem as if he is endorsing our efforts, even when we have gone astray.

One of the many gifts of the Holy Spirit is discernment (read 1 Corinthians 12:1-11 for some others), this gift will help to keep us on track and filter out distractions, good as well as bad, aimed at leading us off course. If you are in doubt or concerned that you are not totally doing what God has called you to do, do not fear, he will quickly get you back on track if you will earnestly seek him in prayer, for he delights in blessing his children and will in no way reject a repentant heart.

Chapter 7

Not having come this way before

One of my biggest struggles as a Christian is applying the word in my life in areas where I have become self-reliant. From very early on in my life, I prided myself as someone who could take care of himself and that included financially. From around the age of eleven I felt the need to earn my own money doing a milk round at weekends. I know that my experiences are similar to many children of my generation who did various, similar part-time jobs such as paper rounds, working in shops etc.

It taught me many valuable lessons which helped to form my perspective on how to achieve success and attain wealth in today's society; find a job, work hard and earn as much as you can so as to enjoy life. However, there is a clear distinction as to what constitutes 'productive' work as it relates to the kingdom of heaven, in comparison to worldly wealth.

After a long period of seeking to be obedient and trust God for my provision, I constantly found myself not totally at rest, wrestling with what I had to do, as opposed to trusting God to provide. It was on a particular day on my way to the dentist, fearful of the cost, knowing that the treatment could be expensive and funds being low, that I began in earnest a serious meditation on God's financial provision.

Two Bible verses were uppermost in my mind, one from Psalms and the other from the book of Jeremiah. In the Psalm the foreknowledge of God was placed before me '...*all the days ordained for me were written in your book before one of them came to be*' (Psalm 139:16 NIV). God specifically makes mention of his knowledge of Jeremiah before he was even born very clear when he says, "*Before I formed you in the womb I knew you, before you were born I set you apart; I appointed you as a prophet to the nations.*" (Jeremiah 1:5 NIV). These verses are rich in meaning and helped to challenge me, whilst also giving me some valuable insights regarding the sovereignty of God, and his involvement not only in our creation, but preparation of our life and work to be done here on earth.

Now whether I reasoned these verses or was led by the Spirit, I don't know, but I concluded that God who created me and knows each day of my life, from beginning to end, would also make full provision for me each day, being the author of my life. I felt a sense of agreement in my heart that this was true. However, this feeling did not last long, as while I was pondering the matter on my way to the dentist, a middle aged man walking in the opposite direction was in conversation on a mobile phone, and as he went past me I heard him say to the person on the other end of the line '...you have to work because you need money to pay your bills...'

As he went on his way I looked up knowing that he had expressed what my fear was, I need to pay my bills, which I believe and know is scriptural. We are to work and make a contribution to our family and the wider community. By now I had arrived at the dentist not sure what to expect, given the fact that I had had recurring problems for over twelve years, which is why they called me in specially to see one of their top consultants, who, unknown to me, was also the owner of the practice.

I approached the reception desk expecting to be asked the usual questions and fill in the forms, however, the usual protocols and questions were waived and I was greeted with a lovely smile from the receptionist and told not to go to my usual waiting room, which is on the first floor, but to the top of the building, as they were expecting me and would call me shortly.

Arriving at the top of the building I saw a welcome sight, two chairs outside of the dental surgeon's room. I promptly sat down, I had only been there a couple of minutes when a dental nurse came up the stairs and seeing me sat down there, smiled, and said I should go into the waiting room, which was opposite where I was sitting. Funny I thought, in all the years I've been coming here I never knew that there was another waiting room.

As I went in I quickly noticed how plush the décor was, compared to where I normally waited on the first floor. This had comfortable leather seats, lovely flooring and a big flat-screen television, water fountain and a coffee table with up-to-date magazines and the daily newspapers. Wow, this is nice I thought. Then, as I reclined in one of the leather chairs with a cup of chilled water in hand, I pondered how pleased I was just to see those two chairs as I reached the top of the building, not realising that this grand provision was here and had been available to me.

The question I was forced to ask myself became, could I do God's will and totally rely on him to take care of all my needs? Like this plush waiting room which I had no knowledge of, has God already made provision for me which I know nothing about that he desires for me to enjoy?

Could it be that my idea of what 'work' really is, be a hindrance to my faith and the reason I found it difficult to trust God in this area. Jesus said *'My food (nourishment) is to do the will (pleasure) of Him who sent Me and accomplish and completely finish His work'* (John 4:34 Amplified Bible). Even when reciting the Lord's Prayer we ask that, the 'Lord's *'…will be done, on earth as it is in heaven…'* (Matthew 6:10 NIV).

I have heard it said many times that where God guides he provides. However, saying it is one thing, but to walk in it is not that easy. I knew that one way or another, to develop in character as a Christian and be productive in the *'…good works, which God prepared in advance for us to do'* (Ephesians 2:10 NIV), I was going to have to cross that bridge of doubt which requires me to turn away from being dependent on my own abilities and understanding and trust God totally on a daily basis. I also realised that my concept of 'work' and priorities regarding what constitutes productive 'labour' would be challenged, as will yours.

When I saw the consultant he made it very clear that he had studied my file and was aware of the problems I had experienced in the past. He also explained in detail the cause of my problem and how he could rectify it. He made it quite clear to me that if I had a problem at any time, to make an appointment and I would be seen immediately, as a priority patient at no extra cost until the work was completed satisfactorily. I can't tell you how this made me feel. The relief of just knowing that this level of service was available to me any time if I had a problem, at no extra cost, really put my mind at ease.

Shortly afterwards I thought, if this is how a mere man can make me feel if I have a problem with a tooth, how much more can God, who loves me, continually put my mind at ease regarding any problem, given the fact that the earth is the Lord's and everything in it.

The access to immediate treatment given to me by the owner of the dental practice, is a picture which reminds me constantly of the access obtained for me by Jesus into God's presence, confident in the knowledge that our position in Christ affords us a different view of life and troubles, with heavenly resources available to comfort, and encourage us to continue in the faith. As Christians we are all invited to '...*come boldly unto the throne of grace, that we may obtain mercy, and find grace to help in time of need...*' (Hebrews 4:16 KJV).

This experience constantly helps to remind me that Jesus invites us to take time to rest in him from the troubles we experience. This will be different for each and every one of us and will vary daily. The promise of experiencing God in the midst of our troubles is a gift to each and every believer, whether we choose to enjoy it or not. Once we have committed our plans to the Lord and are about his business, whether we like it or not, he will provide.

Some of you may be asking yourself why wouldn't I like it? Well, when God provides he does so in his own way and at the appropriate time. My old ways of providing may still be used to some extent, but God's way of providing may well humble us which could challenge a root of pride within us that has developed in our hearts after many years of doing things our way, with us taking credit. God's way means God gets the glory; there is no boasting except in God.

At the moment we gave our lives to Christ he likewise committed heaven's resources to us, this is what I believe Jesus was trying to communicate to his disciples, which includes us, in the Sermon on the Mount when he said '...*do not worry about your life...*' (Matthew 6:25 NIV). Your declaration of faith in Christ was also a declaration of dependence on him, not only to be cleansed of your sins, past, present and future, but it was the doorway to your present and eternal blessings.

Nothing hurts me more at times than knowing that I have the resources and knowledge that can benefit my children, only to watch them choose to struggle and experience difficulty, just for the sake of asking for my help or advice. Let us not be like that. This access we have cost God dearly, it is not just a privilege for us, it blesses the heart of God when we make full use of our birthright and new position as heirs of grace.

Jesus knew that he had to make his disciples realise that to serve God fully, at some point they were going to have to make the will of God a priority in their lives and trust that God would provide everything else they needed, while they were attending to kingdom business. We likewise still have much work to do today, many brothers and sisters who have died in faith have gone on to be with the Lord. Not all of them have seen their prayers for family members, friends etc., answered; their hope has been transferred to those willing to serve God, the body of Christ here on earth.

God's love far outweighs ours in every area, he loves our wives, husbands, children, father, mother, brother, sister, anyone dear to us, much more than we do. He even loves us more than we love ourselves. The passion and desire he has to love us we can only imagine. In a marriage, for example, love has moments when it can be intense, but maintaining that level of pleasure and intensity would be difficult, if not impossible. God's love is pure, constant and all consuming.

The joy and intensity he experienced at the beginning of your new life with him has not changed on his part. We become fearful and doubt, but his love never wanes, wearies of your presence, hearing your voice or listening to your prayers. We do our Lord a disservice when we neglect such a lover and friend who in Psalm 37:4, invites us to delight in him so that he can bless us with the desires of our hearts. Desires he knows we have which can only be fulfilled by him.

To experience this is to truly experience heaven on earth, a secret place in times of trouble. We are never going to be able to escape the daily consequences of living in a fallen world, with its three arch enemies to our peace, described by many a preacher as, the lust of the flesh, the lust of the eyes and the pride of life. However, our intimate time with God in close communion frees us from feeling condemned.

Many times we will have to approach God purely on the basis of his mercy and grace, knowing in our hearts that even on our worst day God declares us righteous and will not turn us away when we seek him, but rather like the prodigal son, who when the father saw him afar off - ran to greet him.

Chapter 8

'...let's talk about sex...'

Many ministers refrain from talking much about the subject of sex and physical intimacy. This is something I totally understand given the potential for their words to be misinterpreted and used as a license to commit sin, or seen as offensive to the sensitivities of church members who believe that this 'sort of thing' should not be discussed. Whatever our view, the Bible calls sexual intercourse between a man and a woman 'natural relations' (Romans 1:26-27). The world on the other hand has no problem discussing the subject loudly, everyday. There are messages going out from the television, radio, advertising and many other sources that are affecting our society in many adverse ways and we as Christians, are not immune. Statistics show that the level of sexual infidelity and divorce amongst Christians is the same as for non-Christians.

Even while writing this book, this chapter was the one I deliberated over the longest as to whether or not it should be included, with a question mark as to whether I should even attempt to broach the subject in writing. However, after listening to one of my favourite radio programmes and hearing a letter read out on air from a female listener and hearing about her struggles in the area of sexual desire and feeling guilty about not being pleasing to God, I knew I had to write something, in the hope that those who are feeling the same way would be reassured about how much we are loved in the midst of our physical desires, changing emotions, and sexual frustrations.

To advance in the kingdom of heaven free from guilt in this way, a clear distinction needs to be made between the physical and the spiritual. Some things that cause the greatest frustration amongst Christians are biological and happen routinely as part of the body's natural functions. Most men will experience spontaneous erections during the early hours of the night and in the morning; this is most commonly due to 'reflex stimulation' of a full bladder, likewise, a women's nipples may also become erect when she is cold and her body is trying to preserve heat.

Even when these bodily functions associated with arousal are stimulated, the cause may still be biological. Wet dreams, which is more prevalent among young men than women has caused many to feel guilty of immorality, especially if the dream involved feelings or actions that the individual would not normally be engaged in, yet during the dream found pleasurable to the point of climax. In young men the build-up of semen in the testicles is routinely the cause of these nocturnal emissions. Moreover, for some woman the second week after her menstruation cycle increases her levels of testosterone along with a greater desire for sexual intimacy.

When we try to control these things solely from a spiritual perspective we find ourselves in the midst of a repeating dilemma in which we feel constantly defeated and to be failing God. We are fearfully and wonderfully made and in this section these positive elements of who we are will be explored from the male and female perspective, while shining a little light into how and why we feel and act the way we do, as well as the natural sexual impulses associated with arousal.

In the classic book The Sexual Side of Marriage, first published in Great Britain in 1932, Dr Exner gives men an insight into what may be causing conflict in their relationship, and possibly yours:

> '...in most women desire comes in a more or less well-defined tidal variation which is related to the menstrual cycle. Men do not experience periodic variation in sexual desire. Therefore, if they are ignorant of the existence of an ebb and flow rhythm in women, it is difficult for them to understand what seems to them merely variation in temperamental mood. Much friction and unhappiness arise out of this situation...'

> p67

Our sexual appetite is very hard to define and unique. Some will have a higher demand for physical intimacy than others. For some this will vary over time with age, for others it may remain the same, if not increase. This is perfectly normal. Our sexual desire is influenced by many external factors related to our emotions that affect the way we feel.

Men and women are entering the kingdom of heaven every day, many have been active sexually, unaware that they were doing anything wrong. God meets each and every one of us exactly where we are. To grow in faith we have to accept this, and truly believe that all our sins have been forgiven, past, present and future. The 'Spirit of adoption' by which we call God Father should be a great comfort to all of us. The picture is a beautiful one if you can grasp its meaning. As previously mentioned, when a child is being adopted, the prospective family are normally fully briefed as to the child's history and problems. However, they are only focused on how much they want to love that child. God knows everything about us and chose us in Christ to be adopted into his family, forever. His love and understanding is far greater than any earthly parent could offer.

As children of God, we will have good days and bad days. At times we will feel as if we are not growing at all. We will on occasions even sin deliberately out of fear, frustration or confusion. It is at times like these that we must fully realise that we are still a child of God and go to our Father, fully assured that he will in no way reject a penitent heart that seeks him. He will never reject you.

The parable of the prodigal son is familiar to many, even non-Christians, and is a picture of God's attitude to us as soon as we turn to him. The son had lived a wild and care free life after leaving home and indulged in many pleasures thinking that they would never end. However, once his money had finished, the cold reality of false friendships and life without money soon caused him to grieve leaving his father's house. At a time when he was at his lowest, hungry and having no one to give him anything, the Bible says he *'came to his senses'* and said *'...I will set out and go back to my father...'*

When we find ourselves feeling guilty over some action, thoughts or whatever it may be that is causing stress, we should always remember that we too can go to our heavenly Father. The enemy would tell you that you cannot, that you have gone too far, but these are all lies intended to make you feel condemned and a second class citizen of heaven.

Given all that the prodigal son had done, look at his father's response to him coming home '*But while he was still a long way off, his father saw him and was filled with compassion for him; he ran to his son...*' (Luke 15). When we do not turn to our heavenly Father in prayer after our moments of weakness, we carry unnecessary burdens that rob us of our joy. The father's response in this parable conveys a beautiful message of acceptance, even after we have fallen short of what we know to be God's best.

The Bible says '*he ran*' and our heavenly Father is keen for us to come to him during these times also, to free us from the burden of guilt and gently restore us with his love. To advance in the kingdom of heaven you will have to learn how to apply this principle, sometimes daily. Once you have given it to God, leave it with him and move on, your time will be better spent focusing on doing what you know he wants you to do, than dwelling on past failures. Such actions may seem spiritual, but if practised on a regular basis can prove invaluable for the believer. Try to quickly learn from your mistakes, and use them as a source for future prayers for God to strengthen and help you cope wisely with similar trials in the future.

Unfulfilled desire

The essence of a healthy marriage is good communication coupled with a healthy sex life, where both partners feel able to express their sexual desires in a way that enables each to experience intimacy, which strengthens the bond between them, while releasing them from all fears and doubts of being unloved.

This unique bond between a husband and wife, I believe, should also improve with age, making both feel less vulnerable to any form of unwanted intrusion into their relationship that would cause emotional hurt or the pain of rejection, but rather both partners should feel more able to explore their passions in a way that is edifying.

This however, is not the experience of many. The fault lines are all too evident and attempts to repair any cracks, if not handled with great sensitivity can lead to further problems. As a counsellor, I regularly speak with a married person who has on their own volition decided that the time for sex in their marriage has passed, even though they are physically able.

They react with bewilderment when I ask them how their partner took their decision, stating that it has nothing to do with their other half. The conversation then continues with them telling me all about their partner's faults, followed by questions as to why their partner has become so unloving and acting erratically.

When I ask them if there could be a possible link with their decision to refrain from any form of sexual contact, they continue to profess that it is their decision and nothing to do with their partner, at which point I have to point out that scripture does not support that viewpoint: *'The wife's body does not belong to her alone but also to her husband. In the same way, the husband's body does not belong to him alone but also to his wife. Do not deprive each other except by mutual consent and for a time...'* (1 Corinthians 7:4-5)

The situation may well have been developing for months, in some cases years, where any sexual advances are ruthlessly and radically repelled, in such an aggressive manner, that it would cause Attila the Hun to reconsider his options. This is not to say that there are legitimate circumstances, through ill health or long term separation, where a partner will need to be more imaginative as to how sexual fulfilment can be achieved. Through open and frank discussions however, agreements can be reached to each partner's mutual benefit.

A constant review as to where each partner is sexually needs to form part of the marriage to ascertain how not to let this vital part of the relationship flounder through neglect or false assumptions, especially as our bodies change or become incapacitated in some way, due to injury or long term sickness. The Lord is not embarrassed about sex and neither should we be, include God in your prayers when seeking how to improve things and overcome obstacles to your mutual pleasure.

This is not to say that we are to be ready and willing for sex 24/7, we all have variances in our desires and that includes moments where we need to be affirmed through sexual fulfilment. These feelings may arise simultaneously with your partner, or it may be a time when you are indulging them, or you need to be indulged, either way the emphasis is on pleasing each other for the benefit of your marriage, such selfless giving always yields fruits of joy that can sustain you both through the difficult times.

Before I go any further I want to be clear that I am not advocating that we should ever allow ourselves to be subjected to any form of abuse or actions that are known to violate scriptural principles on love and marriage, which is founded on mutual love and respect. Where there is abuse, appropriate measures should be taken to prevent harm to oneself and family, this is crucial.

An article was sent to me from the agony column of Christianity Magazine with the heading, 'Can I divorce my abusive husband?' and addressed to Dear Maggie. The author was a married woman with three children who was experiencing verbal abuse from a recovering alcoholic and drug taking husband, who had also admitted to being unfaithful on more than one occasion. The situation had become so bad that she was desperate for some relief and divorce seemed to be the only option as she says '…I no longer feel I can live with being made to feel like I am a bit of dirt he picked up on his shoes.'

Maggie's response to the reader's letter was clear and I believe correct:

'…On several fronts, therefore, according to scripture, I believe you are free to leave this marriage if you choose…Your life, mind and body are of infinite value- fearfully and wonderfully made by a caring heavenly father…'

Although this may be an extreme case, the circumstances are not uncommon. However, like the spiritual growth of individuals, the maturing of a marriage and the mystery of two becoming one flesh present some unique challenges for both partners as they lay down previously held beliefs or worldly viewpoints in exchange for a better way of living, guided and supported by scriptural principles.

Healing from past hurts

Some of you reading this may be feeling guilty or feel that you have blown it with regard to your behaviour in your marriage or past relationships, don't worry, it is never too late. The very fact that you are reading this book at this time means that the lessons can still be applied, if not to your life, to someone close to you through your deeper understanding of how to avoid future difficulties. The resurrection spirit of Christ lives in all of us who believe and the Lord can and will make all things new, including past hurts, failures and misplaced desires. This is a time of healing where he will now satisfy our desires with good things that bring us peace and glorify him.

The beauty of the character of God portrayed in Christ through the power of the Holy Spirit is something I continually find amazing. The scriptures should instil in us a real sense of hope and confident assurance that we are loved beyond measure. This realisation in our hearts will not only delight us to do God's will, but also enable us to receive instruction and discipline without feeling rejected or becoming embittered.

God gives every woman biblical insight into the condition of man when referring to Adam in Genesis 2 saying, '...*it is not good for the man to be alone.*' (Genesis 2:18 NIV) Equally, from this verse every man should fully realise his condition of loneliness without the love of a Godly woman to make him whole. The message is two-fold and can bring great blessings to relationships if we are open to receive it and humble enough in our hearts to comfort our partners in a spirit of sacrificial love. How you respond to this God given opportunity is up to you.

All correction by God is done in love for our future benefit and peace and should always lead us into closer fellowship with our heavenly Father. Spurgeon's says that 'God has one Son without sin, but not a single child without the rod' (Morning May 31 Morning and Evening Daily Readings) for Christ himself learnt obedience by the things he suffered.

Those of us who are parents understand that there are times when we have to instruct our children in a way that they may not approve of, purely on the basis that we know what is best and more importantly, the problems that will occur if they follow an ill-advised path. The point I want to try and make here is that our motive is always love for our child. God's love for us is much greater than any human affection and it never wanes, it is from everlasting to everlasting, if you '...*know how to give good gifts to your children, how much more will your Father in heaven...*' (Matthew 7:11).

Finally, I realise that when approaching the subject of sex there are many viewpoints and beliefs on what's permissible, what's not, how much is too much, when and where it should be done, I could go on. Listening to the advice of others can have its benefits, but it can also be very problematic. If you are married, you and your spouse have become one flesh and both of you, either individually, or together, should never be afraid to approach the creator of sex, God himself, when you're in need of counsel in this area.

God is not embarrassed about your sexual desires and passions or the pleasure you give, as well as receive from your partner, make requests for greater pleasure and intimacy a regular part of your prayer life. Ask continually for greater insight and levels of intimacy that will strengthen your marriage. Also include requests for being released from any unnatural fears, attitudes or inhibitions that make you feel guilty or falsely condemned. A greater understanding of your partner's legitimate sexual and emotional needs will not only bless you, but bless your partner too, *'The man and his wife were both naked and they felt no shame.'* (Genesis 2:25 NIV).

Chapter 9

Freedom through forgiveness

'I am forgotten by them as though I were dead; I have become like broken pottery'.

This verse from Psalm 31:12 (NIV) came to me during a time of extreme hardship and personal tragedy. I could not see a way forward and knew I could not go back. In your fight of faith against sin and what you know to be wrong, the above verse may be how the world is making you feel at the moment. However, this is not your true identity and whatever troubles you are facing at the moment can be viewed as temporary and subject to change, even if they have been ongoing. Peace in the midst of any storm is available to you right now for the asking.

No matter how low and despondent you may feel, your position as a child of God still gives you the victory over every trial and tribulation. We must guard against giving way to fear and the deceptions of the enemy, even if we are struggling with confusion as to why God is allowing the situation to continue for so long. It may seem that the enemy has everything going their way, but fret not, Paul says *'...when I am weak then I am strong'* (2 Cor. 12:10).

For me, part of the comfort of receiving Psalm 31:12 was that, through God's word my feelings were being expressed to me in a way that confirmed that the Holy Spirit was fully aware of my situation. The Bible says know the truth and the truth shall set you free; however, sometimes that truth may be rather unpleasant.

Being able to receive the truth without seeking revenge or becoming bitter is an important aspect of our fellowship with God. When God feels able to tell you something difficult or unpleasant on a personal level, he is treating you as a mature Christian, one in whom he can confide. The mistake many of us make, including me in the early days, was to take it upon myself to impose my will or act guided purely by my emotions or feelings of hurt.

One of the names of the Holy Spirit is Comforter. When the verse from Psalm 31:12 *'I am forgotten by them as though I were dead; I have become like broken pottery'*, echoed in my spirit, it conveyed not only how I was feeling at the time, but it let me know that I was not alone. My heart was exposed to someone who knew all too well what I was feeling and could relate to me in my hurt and sorrow as no one else could. This feeling of support and love in the midst of my trouble, enabled me to release my feelings of hurt and confusion in a way that did not make me panic but rest, trusting that God was in full control and not just aware of my pain, but actively involved in my healing.

Before I go any further, I am not saying that we should allow ourselves to accept hostile or unfair treatment. We are to challenge wrong doing and not accept anything that undermines who we are as human beings, created in the image of God. However, life will very often present challenges that have unclear or no readily available solutions and may well cause us to react or respond in a way that puts us in a quandary. In many cases these will indeed be emotive issues with strong feelings and varying points of view on both sides. Times like these are inevitable, what we need to be careful of is making assumptions based on our limited understanding. Wisdom is a good friend and strong partner during such times and something we are all told to pray for continually.

When arguments and dissentions become particularly heated, opposing views and stances become entrenched, with both parties holding so tightly to their own opinions that a lot of talking is being done, but very little listening. The longer this goes on the harder it becomes to resolve the issue, because now not only does no one want to back down, but pride is at stake, as to be proven wrong after so confidently asserting ones position as being right, would be too embarrassing.

This also is a spiritual battle ground the enemy uses to great effect. So often the most long standing grudges between friends or family, which started off with something very trivial and small, has continued for years, due to a reluctance of either party to acknowledge they were wrong, or expecting an apology for a received hurt that was not forthcoming. Over time these roots of bitterness go deeper and deeper into a person's heart, affecting their other relationships, fostering a tendency to constantly be on guard and unable to relax.

Unfortunately, far too many of my counselling sessions are based on this issue, with so many unwilling to forgive, preferring to hold on to past hurts with a form of affection that is comforting to them. In some cases, the very thought of forgiveness makes them become incensed. We all have had experiences which have required us to forgive or be forgiven; there is a blessed hope for us if we can appreciate just what a difference it can make to our daily lives. Corrie Ten Boom puts it this way:

> 'Forgiveness is the key which unlocks the door of resentment and the handcuffs of hatred. It breaks the chains of bitterness and the shackles of selfishness'.

The Bible says that we are to 'forgive our enemies'. We are told to do this because it frees us to live on a higher plain, in fellowship with God who sees the whole picture of any and every situation and is more than capable to resolve it all to our satisfaction. The Bible tells us that, *'The king's heart is in the hand of the Lord… he turns it wherever he will'* (Proverbs 21:1 KJ2000).

God is a righteous judge who loves justice and when we present our case to him by faith, while seeking to maintain our peace, resolving that he knows all things, we are proclaiming the matter as finished and continue to receive the comfort and blessings of children dearly loved by our Father, who will act fairly for all concerned. This is not easy and your prayer time may consist of many gripes and grumbles toward God as to why he allowed the situation. Don't feel guilty as this is a safe place to vent your dissatisfaction in fellowship with God, he knows your hurt so don't try and be 'spiritual' and eloquent praying what you think he wants to hear, be open and honest, he loves you.

The more you practice this the easier it will become to quickly defer a judgment regarding any contentious issue that you find yourself involved in, you will now automatically recognise yourself being lured down a path where pride and resentment reside and quickly respond with honesty and wisdom in such a way that brings peace and healing, rather than throwing fuel on a potentially explosive situation.

God wants all his ambassadors to operate in this world in such a way that when trouble or contentions arise, people are not only pleased that you are present, but seek your advice. When, as Christians, we operate on this level, not being a part of the problem, but rather a part of the solution, God gets the glory, *'Blessed are the peacemakers, for they will be called sons of God'* (Matthew 5:9).

You may be thinking of things done to you which were unfair, or be feeling guilty for some of your own actions, I can think of many examples in my own life, however, if we want to build our lives on a sure foundation and enjoy the peace offered in scripture through forgiveness, then this is one principle that we need to put into practice, we need not only to forgive others, but ourselves.

Once you start to practice this principle, the Fruits of the Spirit will start to manifest themselves throughout every aspect of your life, in ways that you could not imagine, healing past hurts, while guiding you to walk in newness of life that is like rivers of living water nourishing a parched and thirsty world.

God is beholding to no man, so when he asks us to forgive it is ultimately for our own benefit. He loves us so much and has made provision for us who are in Christ to be content in the midst of any and every situation that challenges or confronts us on a daily basis.

Chapter 10

Leisure time a spiritual necessity
(God is in control, even when you're playing tennis)

The idea of pleasure and a walk of faith very seldom come together. We hear a lot about war, the good fight, being living sacrifices and many other truths regarding our lives and the reality of being a Christian. However, that is not all of what makes you, you. The Lord knows that we also need rest every now and then from these struggles. This time of rest can take many forms depending on our gifts and interests. This too should be viewed as a blessing from God which we should also be eager to 'stir up' along with our ministry gifts.

This for me is one area where I have had the greatest battle. My focus was always on achievement and the idea of pursuing an activity purely for pleasure and self-gratification has always been a low priority for me, as I have seen it as a self indulgence. However, I now realise that leisure time, far from being a waste, is absolutely necessary, in fact crucial if we are to maintain a balance and keep a realistic sense of perspective of God's sustaining power.

In every profession there are good days and bad days, in nature we have different seasons with new challenges and blessings. In the book of Ecclesiastes 3:1-4 we are told; '...*There is a time for everything, and a season for every activity under heaven...a time to weep and a time to laugh, a time to mourn and a time to dance...'*

We neglect these leisure times at our own cost. God has created so many wonderful things in this world that he wants us to enjoy. Explore your creative nature; develop a hobby or interest, purely for your enjoyment. This also can become a time of intimate fellowship and thanksgiving to God. The commands of the Lord will challenge us to grow, but they are not burdensome if we realise that he loves us and even our times of enjoyment are a gift from him.

M. Scott Peck in his book The Road Less Travelled, on the subject of hobbies puts it this way:

'...we need to provide ourselves with all kinds of things that are not directly spiritual. To nourish the spirit the body must also be nourished. We need food and shelter. No matter how dedicated we are to spiritual development, we also need rest and relaxation, exercise and distraction. Saints must sleep and even prophets must play.'

p95

For me, this has been a difficult lesson to learn because I felt that if I were to simply enjoy an activity purely for my pleasure, then I must be neglecting something more important, some 'work' that God wants me to do. The reality is God is in total control, even if I am playing tennis (even very poorly, I'm not good at tennis), painting, reading a book, listening to music etc., we all need 'down time' where we become, in a sense, like children again.

As a father I know the joy of teaching my daughters to ride their bikes. The times we had with me holding the back of the bike and them shouting 'don't let go', at first fearful that they might not stay upright, to later on seeing the joy on their faces as they rode around the park laughing, playfully enjoying what they had achieved, filled me with great joy. Can you imagine how much more your heavenly Father will be pleased for you, when you invite him to bless you in this area?

My joy came from the fact that the learning and ability to experience the pleasures of riding a bike was something we did together, my joy was seeing the pleasure on their faces, having successfully overcome their fears. They were always under my watchful eye and protection, even though they did fall off a few times, they were well protected with the right clothing, even the location chosen for their lessons was surveyed beforehand so as to avoid any real hurt. I never deterred them from getting back on and trying again because, even as a child, they knew that once they had overcome this barrier, enjoyment awaited, freedom to ride their bikes at will.

Your heavenly Father wants you to enjoy your life; he sees yours tears of sorrow, hears your prayers and welcomes you to also laugh with him, enjoying intimate fellowship in every area of your life. These times help us to realise that the battle truly belongs to the Lord, who works all things together according to his will. Such times of fun and laughter will add a new dimension to your relationship with God, the same God who walked with Adam, '...*in the cool of the day*' (Genesis 3:8), is the same God who created a garden for him, so richly diverse in all sorts of trees '...*You are free to eat from any tree in the garden*' (Genesis 2:16).

We are all familiar with what happened soon after, but, can you imagine what all the other trees must have looked like? I believe that in each of our lives God has planted beautiful 'trees', good for spiritual, physical and emotional nourishment during our walk with him. The time to seek God is now; he wants you to be healthy in every aspect of your life. The enemy will constantly try to deceive you about your walk and what you are achieving for God. Let God worry about that, our duty is to trust and rely totally on God's full knowledge of us and his power to deliver us from any situation, picking us up when we fall.

To come to God with this attitude in the midst of trials is to embrace true liberty and freedom. The false accusations may continue, but the knowledge that you are truly loved in the dark times can be a profound source of joy, during special times of deep intimacy with God '...*for your Father has been pleased to give you the kingdom...*'' (Luke 12:32)

Bible Study Plan

This is a personal bible study plan to enable you to receive the riches of God's truth. The study plan invites you to read God's word and engage your heart and mind by asking questions and reasoning before reading or listening to a detailed exposition on the scripture.

Always ask yourself by way of reflection what is God saying to me through these verses, for *'All scripture is given by inspiration of God…'*(2 Timothy 3:16 KJV). Example 1 below, gives a guide on how to approach your study of scripture.   I suggest you familiarise yourself with each column.

Example 1

Book: *Example…* **2 Timothy**	**Words/phrases that need clarifying**	**Contextual questions and challenges**	**Based on my own understanding of scripture what do I think they mean?**
Chapter 1:1-18	<u>Verse 11</u> 1)Herald 2)Apostle <u>Verse 14</u> 3)Guard (used twice) **Advanced Study** Word meaning from a bible dictionary or concordance	<u>Verse 2</u> Who is Timothy and why is Paul writing to him? Is he really his son? <u>Verse4</u>…long to see you…? 1)Where is Paul writing from? <u>Verse 9</u> 1)saved us - from what? 2)called us - to what? 3)Holy life?	

Look for Jesus Christ throughout your study as this will help you to engage with the Holy Spirit in fellowship and learning. You will find that the more the Lord leads you through his word, the greater your desire will be to draw near to him. You will automatically want to know more. For example, what does the Bible say about Eunice, Timothy's mother or Phygelus and Hermogenes? What do their names mean? Does my Bible dictionary have any information on them which will help me interpret this passage?

Ask yourself what can you learn about the character and love of God from this passage of scripture and if I was asked to explain it to a non-Christian what would it sound like? What questions might they have? Rehearsing these things in our mind brings us into communion with heaven (meditation).

The final column in Example 1 above is not meant to embarrass you or highlight any lack of knowledge, it will help to prepare your mind to receive the truth of God's word by focusing on and answering specific questions that you can easily recollect and associate with scripture. You may also be surprised at how much you already know, engage and enjoy, God wants you to know him and his ways.

Example 1 above covers chapter 1 of 2 Timothy, however, the same format can be applied to one verse, a character or a situation, depending upon where you feel comfortable and what you are asking God for or seeking to learn. You could even try it for a deeper knowledge of a favourite Psalm.

The questions you ask don't have to be as detailed as in the example. Whatever challenges or excites you in any way, make a note and see what the scriptures say about it, for although commentaries and dictionaries are a great help, the best commentary on the Bible is the Bible.